# Rhythm & Blues
# Song Lyrics

## Brady Kent

# Copyright

2024 Rhythm and Blues Song Lyrics

Author: Brady Kent   © copyright of Brady Kent.
All rights reserved. Published by Brady Kent Books.



**Website**: www.brand.page/bradykentpoet
**E Mail**: www.bradykentpoet@gmail.com
**Soundcloud**: www.soundcloud.com/discover
**LinkedIn**: www.linkedin.com/in/brady-kent
**TikTok**: www.tiktok.com/@bradykent
**Facebook**:www.facebook.com/BradyKentPoet
**X**: www.Brady Kent (@BradykentPoet) / X
**Instagram**: www.instagram.com/bradykentpoet
**YouTube**: www.youtube.com/@Bradykent-d5w

## Preface

'Rhythm & Blues Song Lyrics' is the most
recent addition to the Brady Kent
collection of books.

My mission is to look at subject matter
from a different point of view

Ultimately everything seems to sit nicely
under the Rhythm and Blues banner
Four of my previous song lyrics are being
worked up into songs by experienced song
writers.


Brady Kent

## Also by Brady Kent

Politics and Poems
Sentiments and Poems
Story Telling Song Lyrics
Fire Escape
Improvised Song Lyrics
Frozen Fences
Rhythm and Blues Song Lyrics
Emotions and Song Lyrics

# Contents

# Rhythm & Blues
# Song Lyrics

## Brady Kent

**Kinder to folks**

I'm a distant wantaway, thinking about
tomorrow, never today, kind a guy.

Always leaving. I never say I love her, and
I make cry.

I don't deserve my girl. Why does she
stick around? Never quitting.

I'm a distant wantaway, thinking about
tomorrow, never today, kind a guy.

I'm a leaving, never say I love her, make
her cry, guy.

Oh, why does she stay? It's always just
one way......mmmmm

Why does she feel like this, why do we
kiss? Mmmmm

I'm a distant wantaway, thinking about
tomorrow, never today, kind a guy.

Walks into a room, eyes follow her. Why is
she with that mean old poser?

Time to face my truth. I want to stay with
my sweetheart lover.

I'm a distant wantaway, thinking about tomorrow, never today, kind a guy.

I'm a leaving, never say I love her, make her cry, guy.

A distant wantaway guy.

A never say I love her, make her cry guy.

# Bend the throttle

I know we quarrelled, but we can take on
the world.

oooo

Love you baby, I worked hard to get my
own place.

But I wanna to take a chance, feel the
wind on my face?

What do we have to lose, let's just be
true.

Giving it all up, to start anew, just to be
with you.

I know we quarrelled, but we can take on
the world.

Come on baby, together we can strike out.

'I'm coming with you' is what I wanna
hear.

Let's get in the car and drive, with no fear.

Its late but let's getta outta town tonight.

I know we quarrelled, but we can take on the world.

Let's figure it out, and move out.

The city is behind us. Its red lights all the way.

We're going south to God knows where. Wherever we stray.

It feels right together. Like we're made for each other

I know we quarrelled, but we can take on the world.

So right together. Like we're made for each other

I know we quarrelled, but we can take on the world.

We can take on the world.
We can take on the world.

oooo

# A friend that makes me blue

I've got you in view, a friend, that makes
me blue
Other thoughts on my mind, but you keep
coming back. I can't leave you behind.
I love you, but no one knows. I won't even
admit it to myself, won't ever let it show.

I've got you in view, a friend, that makes
me blue.
You wouldn't understand, I would drive
you crazy. It wouldn't go as planned
I'm never going to win. You know me, but
you don't know my dream.

I've got you in view, a friend, that makes
me blue.
We've got to get out of town, so I can to
tell you how I feel. To see if you want to
be more. To see if my longing heart can
heal.

I've got you in view, a friend, that makes
me blue.
It's too late to plea. Maybe it's time to cry.
Maybe it was never going to be. Guess in
always on standby.

I've got you in view, a friend, that makes
me blue. Makes me blue...oooo

**Hey Jane**

Hey Jane, we've got to stop meeting like this. If you want more, let's say goodbye with a kiss.

Husband Joe is goanna find out; it won't be worth the fallout.

It's just not right, you've got a kid.

The hotel room is taken, for only one person.

Hey Jane, we've got to stop meeting like this. If you want more, we need to say goodbye with a kiss.

I think we've been seen. They know where you've been.

Next time we must be sure. Go way out of town, be more careful.

Hey Jane, we've got to stop meeting like this. If you want more, let's say goodbye with a kiss

There is no future for us. We both know what this is and is not.

Husband Joe is goanna find out; it won't be worth the fallout.

If you want more, let's say goodbye with a kiss.

Hey Jane, we've got to stop meeting like this. If you want more, let's say goodbye with a kiss.

## I'm down so low


If the new baby is my son?
Why the hell the visit from the ex-
husband.

She got pregnant; I was happy.
Doctors asks me, am I the Daddy?

Already a six-year-old daughter,
Not ready for a surprise extra

No call to say, she was in labour.
Cards received, but no love for me

If the new baby is my son?
Why the hell the visit from the ex-
husband.

Missed the birth, she says it's mine.
Can I believe her this time.

The parents dont approve of me.
Jesus, he don't even look like me

Claims it's mine, not sure I can believe
her. Kids don't always relate to each other

If the new baby is my son?
Why the hell the visit from the ex-
husband.

Claims it's mine, nut sure I can believe
her. Kids don't always relate to each other

If the new baby is my son?
Why the hell the visit from the ex-
husband.

## Imposter

Who am I kidding, no one is fooled. This is
not living. I'm a joke, a guy that's
ridiculed.

I go from girl to girl, but never create a
life. Just like the song, I'm the 'great
pretender', I'll never find a wife.

No one is fooled, just like my father.
I'm no better, I'll end up like him, a lonely
loser.

It's all about me, it's all about number
one. Wasting my life, chasing another for
fun.

Alone and abandoned, nowhere to go
No one to love, or be loved back, nothing
to show.

No one is fooled, just like my father.
I'm no better, I'll end up like him, a lonely
loser.

My first love will always claim, 'he's crazy,
doesn't know what he wants, he just
playing the game'.

My last love would say, 'I have finally had
enough, I can't go on this way, for one
more day'

No one is fooled, just like my father.
I'm no better, I'll end up like him, a lonely
loser.

The rest in between will laugh and say' he
knows he will end up old and lonely
someday'.

Everyone betrayed, just like my father.
Living alone, fast becomes slow.
No one left, a weak and fake hero.

No one is fooled, just like my father.
I'm no better, I'll end up like him, a lonely
loser.

I'll end up like him, a lonely loser.

## Its time Baby

Let's fool around, let's not waste time.
I need your body to combine with mine.

Talk to me, tell me what you want. Tell
me, should I stay silent?

Hey baby lets go deep, turn around. Going
down low, down on the ground.

Let's fool around, let's not waste time.
I need your body to combine with mine.

Playing our music to be in the mood, 'Let's
Get It On' or 'Nice and Slow', feels good.

This time slow and precise, let's savour
the time. Let's stay in paradise.

Let's fool around, let's not waste time.
I need your body to combine with mine.

Let's go again, your curving outward. Your
kisses are sweet, I'm yours, I'm complete.

No talk, no sleep no, no more. Let me look
at you, entwined and raw.

Let's fool around, let's not waste time.
I need your body to combine with mine.

## Man, you look good

Your long brown hair, wild and free.
I love your dark blue eyes, your mystery.

On your own. Never see any fear.
There no way you will stay alone.

In the same room, I feel like a fool,
whilst you're just kinda cool.

Your long brown hair, wild and free.
I love your dark blue eyes, your mystery.

So good, more I could say. How do I talk
to you, love you someday?

Know my name? We met on the balcony,
cold from the sea breeze.

Your long brown hair, wild and free.
I love your dark blue eyes, your mystery.

I'll say you're beautiful if I dare. Say what
to make you care?

I always wonder. My all the time
mysterious lover.

Your long brown hair, wild and free.
I love your dark blue eyes, your mystery.

Your long brown hair, wild and free.
Dark blue eyes, my unsolved mystery.

## The black mood blues

In in a black mood, just like those other desperate fools.

No defence I can think of, nothing to un cover. No reasons, ever!

Its black, I'm mean really black. It's the black mood blues, they keep coming back.

In in a black mood, just like those other desperate fools.

I've tried drink, I've tried a pill, but they don't stop the black mood devil.

It's never going away, despite what they say. Maybe I should run away.

In in a black mood, just like those other desperate fools.

How black can black get? Can I still turnback?

I don't use the 'S' word, Maybe I should. So, my pleas will be heard.

In in a black mood, just like those other desperate fools

Its black, I'm mean really black. It's the
black mood blues, they keep coming back.

## Red wine and gold

Red wine for crazy thoughts. Gold for
fearnoughts.

We're not getting old; we are not facing
pain. Let's just stay in control.

Age is not a bad of honour, let's agree to
always stay younger.

Let's not talk about time. Nor the time we
both have left to climb.

Red wine for crazy thoughts. Gold for
fearnoughts.

Let's go baby, let's be extreme. Let's jump,
let's swim and scream.

The time of our lives with time to spare.
No excuses, but to try and dare.

Red wine for crazy thoughts. Gold for
fearnoughts.

Red wine and gold that glistens.
We've gotta the distance.

Let's jump, let's swim and scream.

## Smart girl, pre loved

No longer in pain, she's open at last.
Some guy needs the courage, to reach out
and ask.

She won't do the running; she's burnt
from the past. She a pre loved girl, from a
time that's passed.

Cool, one of a kind, a girl who doesn't
need to show, doesn't want to know.

She doesn't flirt, she doesn't put herself
out there. You gotta do the running, gotta
do more than stare.

Air conditioned and composed. A smart
girl with options, but hardnosed.

A pre-loved girl that's may be looking for
more. To go again with a guy, that melts
her core.

Cool, one of a kind, a girl who doesn't
need to show, doesn't want to know.

No longer in pain, she's open at last.
Some guy needs the courage, to reach out
and ask.

Cool, one of a kind, a girl who doesn't
need to show, doesn't want to know.

## Rapping and drinking

We ain 't tired, we ain 't poor, were in the
hood, listening to Mr Gaye, live on tour.

Keep on drinking all day long. Don't stash
the cash, don't say it's wrong.

We ain 't tired, we ain 't poor, were in the
hood, listening to Mr Gaye, live on tour.

We ain 't tired, we ain 't poor, were in the
hood, listening to Mr Gaye, live on tour.

We never sleep, we never eat, always
ready to go, ready for ass, but not to
keep.

Use your tongue to speak out loud, back
your boys, stand loud and proud.

We ain 't tired, we ain 't poor, were in the
hood, listening to Mr Gaye, live on tour.

F.... our enemy. The life we've chosen, it's
our mother f....... destiny.

Staying here, no back up support. Rags to
rags, ain 't no riches they don't import.

We ain 't tired, we ain 't poor, were in the
hood, listening to Mr Gaye, live on tour.

Hash in the ghetto, smoking dope in the
den. F...... tomorrow, every hour until then.

Don't try to understand it all, the hood got
the best of me, I'm still drinking y'all.

We ain 't tired, we ain 't poor, were in the
hood, listening to Mr Gaye, live on tour.

We never sleep, we never eat, always
ready to go, ready for ass, but not to
keep.

Were ready for ass, but not to keep,
listening to Mr Gaye, live on tour.

## Don't be alone

Alone. Like the dead in Flanders Fields.  A
cause no one remembers, or pleads.

For you, my love the years have passed,
since you desired another in place of me

Alone on my own, it's always been, part of
my legacy, the end of a dream.

Alone. Like the dead in Flanders Fields. For
a cause that no one remembers, or
pleads.

Thirty years wasted, easy to say. No way
back. I cried every day.

I want to die alone. So, my body is not
found for days, so saying good bye is
delayed.

Alone. Like the dead in Flanders Fields. For
a cause that no one remembers, or
pleads.

I've died already. My physical end brings
relief. I still crave the cease with no grief.

Alone. Like the dead in Flanders Fields. For
a cause that no one remembers, or
pleads.

For you, my love the years have passed,
since you desired another in place of   me

Alone since you desired another in place
of, me

Alone. Like the dead in Flanders Fields. For
a cause that no one remembers, or
pleads.

## What did JLo say to Matt?

Hey Matt how you doing, what happening?
Ben and I have split, he's gone back to
acting.

We ain 't been right for a while, don't take
any notice of my PR smile.

Looks like Bens met someone new.
Hanging with a Kennedy girl in Beverley
Hills.

Daughter of RFK, he's never going to be
president. She loves beer and smoking,
but there no resentment.

We ain 't been right for a while, don't take
any notice of my PR smile.

Ben says 'were not dating'. The press
says, 'they are intimate but not in
romantic way'

I know you're his best friend, but after two
years we are divorcing, it's the end.

We ain 't been right for a while, don't take
any notice of my PR smile.

Ben is sullen and selfish, with a real big
mouth. It's not true I'm fame obsessed, or
I like the public to know I'm distressed.

We ain 't been right for a while, don't take
any notice of my PR smile.

You know me Matt.

It's not been right for a while, don't take
any notice of my PR smile.

If the press asks, don't say what you
discussed with J Lo.

**Burlesque, oh yea!**

Oh Dita, are you wearing your red corset.

I don't need caricature; I don't need
travesty or parody.

I don't need variety or a theatrical
extravaganza.

No, it's striptease for me baby, and I mean
tease.

Oh Dita, are you wearing your red corset.

If there are erotic moves, I'll stay, like 'All
That Jazz' and 'Cabaret'.

Let's hit the clubs and dance. Le Sandal,
The Blue Angel, for a performance.

Stylish, sexy and crazy super sensual.
Beguiling to both women and men

Oh Dita, are you wearing your red corset

Songs by Christina Aguilera, Dita to tease.
Showtime striptease, and I mean tease.

Oh Dita, are you wearing your red corset.
A Basque Clincher. A Lingerie Bustier.
A Moulin Rouge Boned shaper outfit.

## Can't get past the fling


Like a thorn stuck deep in my heart, your betrayal stings

A constant reminder of the pain you bring

I can't escape the memory, the haunting sight

Of you with her, stealing away the night


Can't get past the fling, it's a heavy weight

A burden I must bear, come what may

Your deception cuts deep, a wound that won't heal

I'm trapped in this cycle, a prisoner of your deceit


Resentment burns within, a fire hard to quench

Your lies and games, a cruel, heartless wrench

You shattered my trust, like a fragile vase that can't be mended

My heart is broken, my spirit's wounded

I need to let go of the past, to find peace within

To break free from the chains that bind me to sin

To forgive and forget, to start anew

And find the strength to rise above the blue


Can't get past the fling, it's a heavy weight

A burden I must bear, come what may

Your deception cuts deep, a wound that won't heal

I'm trapped in this cycle, a prisoner of your deceit

**How are you really**


Tell me darling what do you really feel.
It's years since we did cartwheels!

I just wanna know you're ok. That you
don't dream of flying away.

I just want your light to be bright, to
make sure everything is just right.

Tell me darling what do you really feel.
It's years since we did cartwheels!

Weve not talked for some time, I'm there
for you, you're my perfect rhyme.

I'm there for you if you have the time.
You're my world, I hope your still mine.

Tell me darling what do you really feel.
It's years since we did cartwheels!

You've gone quiet baby. Tell me what's
wrong. I'm out of my mind going crazy.

As long as we keep trying, there's more.
We can stop fighting and keep rising.

Tell me darling what do you really feel.
It's years since we did cartwheels!

I can't believe what you're saying, what
you really feel, so no more cartwheels?

## Heroin Chic look

Don't call the cops, just roll with it.
She's at a gig in cherry red lipstick

Dont worry it's her heroin chic look,
they just try to mimic.

'Skinny worship' rages on, it's in the book.

Don't call the cops, just roll with it.
She's at a gig in cherry red lipstick

Crop tops and low-rise jeans.

Fashion queen, she likes to be seen.

Erratic, with a flair for the dramatic.

Don't call the cops, just roll with it.
She's at a gig in cherry red lipstick

Change, a new look amongst the street
life.

Don't call the cops, just roll with it.

Show a little gratitude, she's got a new
mood.

Don't call the cops, just roll with it
Don't call the cops, just roll with it
Just roll with it…….

Don't call the cops, just roll with it.
She's at a gig in cherry red lipstick

Don't call the cops, just roll with it.
She's at a gig in cherry red lipstick

## Daisy Loo

I'm going crazy, crazy for you lady Daisy
Loo. Oh, and you are so pretty too.

I'm going crazy, crazy for you Daisy Loo.
Dreaming, I was so happy with you.

I've not seen you much lately.  I'm sorry,
you got no cause to be so fiery.

It's gone on for too long Daisy, what did I
do wrong?

I'm going crazy, crazy for you lady Daisy
Loo. Oh, and you are so pretty too.

Are you still my honey Daisy, all dressed
up, looking fine and lacy?

Our time together was so easy Daisy.
Don't let it pass by

Daisy Loo, your one jazzy hippy. It's all
gone crazy, I don't know what to do.

I'm going crazy, crazy for you lady Daisy
Loo. Oh, and you are so pretty too.

**Driving out of town**

I'm driving out of town, so my tax doesn't
get paid. I'm looking for a better life,
looking for a better way.

I'm now in hot Arizona, near that big old
canyon. You're on my mind, it's my old
ways that I'm trying to abandon.

I've reached Flagstaff, deep into the
Apache Sate. My mind drifts back to you,
will you still wait?

I'm heading for Tucson, to find a new job.
Something that keeps me ahead, keeps
me on top.

I'm driving out of town, so my tax doesn't
get paid. I'm looking for a better life,
looking for a better way.

I'll call you girl when I'm ready, I'll ask you
to come to me. I'll be Tucson, Arizona.
I'll be a new man, just you wait and see.

I'm driving out of town, so my tax doesn't
get paid. I'm looking for a better life,
looking for a better way.

I'm looking for a better way, I just need to
get better pay. I just need to get better
pay.

# I got all the blame

It went wrong, I got all the blame. I was
never good enough; I won a lucky
wildcard game.

Yep, I might have tried harder, I might
have been a better partner.

But what the hell, you made my life a
misery. I couldn't wait to get away.

It went wrong, I got all the blame. I was
never good enough; I won a lucky
wildcard game.

You changed into a fighting woman,
someone that wouldn't listen.

You needed your isolation, I needed
conversation.

It went wrong, I got all the blame. I was
never good enough; I won a lucky
wildcard game.

I'm glad it's over; I feel a whole lot better.
Maybe I could have been a better lover.

It went wrong, I got all the blame. I was
never good enough; I won a lucky
wildcard game.

## Why don't you want me?

Why don't you want me, Petra? We once shared pleasure.

You say we talked, that I ignored your wants. It was so long ago; I've forgotten the moment.

You've lost your appetite, your reached an age. You say you 'can't make it right'.

Why don't you want me, Petra? We once shared pleasure.

But you still have needs, you find ways. But not with me, you no longer stay.

'Is there another or not?', you say 'It's not about you, it's about my thoughts.'

Why don't you want me, Petra? We once shared pleasure.

Time has now gone by; we know how this will end. I hope your happy, when were just good friends

Why don't you want me, Petra? We once shared pleasure.

## Trash takes itself out

Leave me, I don't want you around
Leave me, don't turn around.

You know, I'm no longer in pain,
Baby, I'm flying free, I'm free again.

Trash takes itself out

You did no good, no good for me.
You trashed me, left me out in the rain.

Then walked away, to someplace else.
With some guy, to a cheap motel.

Trash takes itself out

But baby you took yourself out,
I'm over you, be in no doubt

Leave me, I don't want you around
Leave me, don't turn around.

Trash takes itself out

Its ok, things have worked out fine,
Your now just a name in a song line.

I'm strong now, and see in front,
I wasted time, I know I shouldn't

Trash takes itself out
Takes itself out.

Leave me, I don't want you around
Leave me, don't turn around.

## Instant heat

In an instant, it needed no touch paper,
No talking, just the heat of danger.

Forget the slow and easy date rule,
We met; we drank we started to fool.

It was hard to stop, hard to contain. In the
dark, on a boat jetty in the pouring rain.

In an instant, it needed no touch paper,
No talking, just the heat of danger.

On the beach, we couldn't stop. Man, you
we were on fire, it was so hot

In an instant, it needed no touch paper,
No talking, just the heat of danger.

Ten years, the rush is still there. It ignites
in an instant, like a glow, like a flare.

In an instant, it needed no touch paper,
No talking, just the heat of danger.

Baby your still mine, your instant heat,
You turn me on, you taste so sweet

In an instant, it needed no touch paper,
No talking, just the heat of danger.

## I will miss our love

Its midnight, too late to tell all.
I will miss our love, a ten second call.

You're looking to choose, hiding your
blues.

Wanta a green light to dance again.
Play the field, with no restrain.

Ten seconds, it's not long, why were we so
wrong.

Its midnight, too late to tell all.
I will miss our love, a ten second call.

It's three o clock, and I can't sleep.  I
guess you wanna make the leap.

Will it wait until morning, need just a few
hours warning

Will it wait until morning, need just a few
hours warning

It's a new day, a new start, you know
you've broken my heart.

Its midnight, too late to tell all.
I will miss our love, a ten second call.

I will miss our love, a ten second call.
I will miss our love, a ten second call

A ten second call